The Great Fire of London

Clare Lewis

raintree
a Capstone company — publishers for children

Raintree is an imprint of Capstone Global Library Limited, a company incorporated in England and Wales having its registered office at 264 Banbury Road, Oxford, OX2 7DY – Registered company number: 6695582

www.raintree.co.uk
myorders@raintree.co.uk

Edited by Clare Lewis
Designed by Steve Mead
Picture research by Kelly Garvin
Production by Victoria Fitzgerald
Originated by Capstone Global Library
Printed and bound in China

ISBN 978 1 4747 1434 1
19 18 17 16 15
10 9 8 7 6 5 4 3 2 1

British Library Cataloguing in Publication Data
A full catalogue record for this book is available from the British Library.

Acknowledgements
We would like to thank the following for permission to reproduce photographs:
Alamy: 19th era, 19, Chronicle, 12; Capstone Press/Peter Bull Art Studio, 8, 9, 16, 17, backcover; Corbis: Blue Lantern Studio, 13, The Print Collector, 20; Getty Images: Guildhall Library & Art Gallery/Heritage Images, 6, Hulton Archive, 10, John Hayls, 22 (left), Time Life Pictures/Mansell/The LIFE Picture Collection, cover, 11; Mary Evans Picture Library, 7, Antiquarian Images, 18, London Fire Brigade Archive, 14; Newscom: Design Pics/Ken Welsh, 22 (right), World History Archive, 5; Shutterstock: Adrian Reynolds, cover (bottom right), peresanz, 4, TTstudio, 21; Wikimedia, 15

Contents

Some words are shown in bold, **like this.** You can
find out what they mean by looking in the glossary.

What was the Great Fire of London?

In 1666, around 350 years ago, a huge fire swept through London. This **monument** stands in London to mark the place where the fire started.

The fire burned for four days. Many buildings were destroyed and people were left homeless. Much of London had to be built again. This is the true story of the Great Fire of London.

What was London like in 1666?

In 1666, London was a busy, crowded city.
The buildings were very close together.
The streets were narrow.

Most of the houses, churches and other buildings were made of wood. Many of them had **thatched** roofs made of straw. The summer of 1666 was long and hot. The buildings and the streets were very dry.

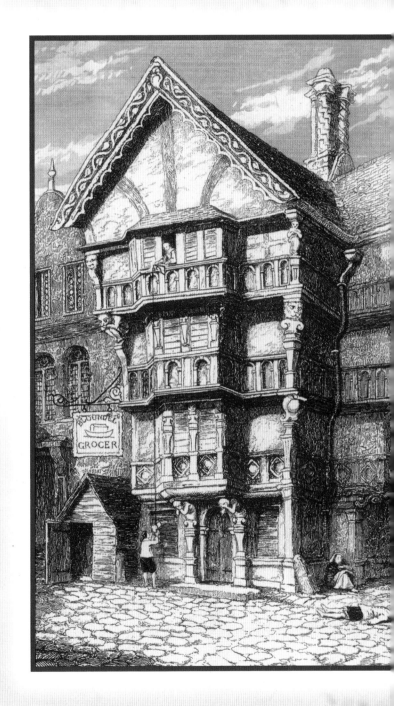

How did the fire start?

Thomas Farriner had a bakery in Pudding Lane. On Sunday 2nd September, he had forgotten to put out the ovens. Just after midnight, a spark dropped out of an oven. The spark started a fire. Soon, the whole building was burning.

Thomas's family lived upstairs. They managed to escape by climbing out of a window and on to a neighbour's roof. Their maid was too scared to climb out. Sadly, she died in the fire.

How did the fire spread?

The fire spread quickly through the narrow streets. Flames leapt easily from one wooden building to the next. A strong wind helped the fire burn even faster. Soon, it was out of control.

The fire spread towards the River Thames. It reached **warehouses** along the river, where lots of oil and **tar** were stored. These burned very easily and at high temperatures.

How did people escape?

Ordinary people had no way of fighting the fire. They grabbed as many belongings as they could and ran for safety.

Many people ran or travelled by cart to the fields around London. From here, they watched as the fire kept on burning.
Lots of people escaped in boats on the River Thames.

How did people try to put the fire out?

There was no proper fire service in 1666.
People tried to put the fire out using
leather buckets and water **squirts**.
They used water from the River Thames.
But the fire was too big.

Fire hooks were used to pull down buildings near the fire. People hoped this would stop the fire spreading. But the fire was moving fast. It quickly spread across the gaps between buildings.

15

How did the fire end?

The fire had been burning for three days.
Then King Charles II ordered his men to
use **gunpowder** to blow up buildings near
the fire. This made bigger gaps between
the buildings to stop the fire spreading.

Finally, on Tuesday, the wind dropped. The firefighters started to gain control. By the morning of Thursday 5th September, the fire was out.

How much of the city was destroyed?

After the fire, the city was in ruins. Around 13,200 houses had been destroyed. St Paul's **Cathedral** and 87 churches were destroyed in the fire. Many people were left homeless.

area destroyed by the fire

Fewer than ten people were reported to have died in the fire. But without their homes, people had to live in tents and shacks on the fields around London. Many more people died in the harsh winter that followed.

19

How was London rebuilt?

It took nearly 50 years for London to be rebuilt. The King said that the new London needed to be safer. He ordered that the new buildings should be made of brick. Streets should be wider with pavements and squares.

The **architect** Christopher Wren designed a new St Paul's **Cathedral**. It was completed in 1711 and is still a famous landmark today.

21

How do we know about the Great Fire?

It sounds very unnaturally here, to have our Nation under ye Patronage of a Dutchman in ye Spanish Court; I wish them neverthelesse good effects from him, since wee have none of our owne Country to Looke out for them there. Pepys.

Dec. 3. 1700.

Samuel Pepys lived in London at the time of the Great Fire. He wrote very detailed diaries about the fire, and how it spread. His diaries describe how people tried to save their belongings by hiding them in churches.

Glossary

architect person who designs buildings

cathedral large church

fire hook long pole with a hook on the end used to pull down buildings

gunpowder powder used in explosions

monument building that helps us remember a person or event

squirt metal tube used for spurting water on a fire

tar thick, dark liquid that comes from coal, used for making roads

thatched having a roof made of straw

warehouse building used to store things

Find out more

Putting on a Play: The Great Fire of London, Tony and Tom Bradman (Wayland, 2015)

The Great Fire of London (Start-up History), Stewart Ross (Franklin Watts, 2014)

The Great Fire of London, Susanna Davidson (Usborne, 2015)

Index